The Last Day
اليوم الآخر

Prepared and translated by
Department of Foreigners' Awareness at Az-Zulfy
إعداد وترجمة
المكتب التعاوني للدعوة والإرشاد وتوعية الجاليات بالزلفي

بالتعاون مع

Legal Rulings Regarding the Last Day

Belief in the Last Day is one of the six fundamental and basic elements of faith. One cannot be a true believer until he believes in what the Qur'an and Sunnah of Allah's Messenger conveyed regarding that day.

Having knowledge about the Last Day and its frequent remembrance is of paramount importance due to its great impact on the reformation of the human soul, its piety, righteousness and steadfastness in the religion of Allah (Islam). Hence, the heart does not become hardened or have the guts to perpetrate acts of disobedience except when it is given to heedlessness with respect to the remembrance of that Day, its horrors and afflictions about which Allah said,

﴿ فَكَيْفَ تَتَّقُونَ إِنْ كَفَرْتُمْ يَوْمًا يَجْعَلُ الْوِلْدَانَ شِيبًا ﴾ [المزمل:١٧]

"Then how can you avoid the punishment, if you disbelieve, on a Day that will make the children grey-headed (i.e. the Day of Resurrection)?" [Al-Muzzammil: 17]

﴿ يَا أَيُّهَا النَّاسُ اتَّقُوا رَبَّكُمْ إِنَّ زَلْزَلَةَ السَّاعَةِ شَيْءٌ عَظِيمٌ * يَوْمَ تَرَوْنَهَا تَذْهَلُ كُلُّ مُرْضِعَةٍ عَمَّا أَرْضَعَتْ وَتَضَعُ كُلُّ ذَاتِ حَمْلٍ حَمْلَهَا وَتَرَى النَّاسَ سُكَارَى وَمَا هُم بِسُكَارَى وَلَكِنَّ عَذَابَ اللَّهِ شَدِيدٌ ﴾

[الحج: ١،٢]

"O mankind! Fear your Lord and be dutiful to Him! Verily, the earthquake of the Hour (of Judgment) is a terrible thing. The Day you shall see it, every nursing mother will forget her nursling and every pregnant one will drop her load, and you shall see mankind as in a drunken state, yet they will not be drunken, but severe will be the Torment of Allah." [Al-Hajj: 1, 2]

The Last Day

Death

It is the end of every living soul in the world. Allah the Most High said,

﴿ كُلُّ نَفْسٍ ذَائِقَةُ المَوْتِ ﴾ [آل عمران: ١٨٥]

"Every soul will taste of death." [Al-Imran: 185]

﴿ كُلُّ مَنْ عَلَيْهَا فَانٍ ﴾ [الرحمن: ٢٦]

"Everyone upon it (the earth) will perish." [Ar-Rahman: 26]

﴿ إِنَّكَ مَيِّتٌ وَإِنَّهُمْ مَيِّتُونَ ﴾ [الزمر: ٣٠]

"Verily, you will die and verily, they (too) will die." [Az-Zumar: 30]

No human being will live forever in this world, as Allah said,

﴿ وَمَا جَعَلْنَا لِبَشَرٍ مِنْ قَبْلِكَ الخُلْدَ ﴾ [الأنبياء: ٣٤]

"And We did not grant to any man before you eternity [on earth]." [Al-Anbiya: 34]

It is worthy to mention the following points:

1. Most people are heedless of death; despite that it is a certain and undoubtable reality. A Muslim should remember death frequently and prepare for it by making provision in this world for his hereafter through righteous deeds before it is too late. The Messenger of Allah said, **"Seize five things before five things; your life before your death, your health before your illness, your leisure time before your busy time, your youth before your old age and your wealth before your poverty."** [Transmitted by Ahmad]

   Remember that the dead do not carry anything of this world with them to the grave. Rather, it is only their deeds that abide with them. So be keen to take the provision of righteous deeds by which you will have eternal bliss and be delivered from the chastisement by the grace of Allah.

The Last Day

2. Man's life span is ambiguous. No one knows it but Allah. Nobody knows when or where he will die because this is part of the knowledge of the unseen, which Allah, the Most Glorified and Exalted, has exclusively kept to Himself.

3. When death comes, it is not feasible to avert, postpone, or flee from. Allah the Most High said,

﴿ وَلِكُلِّ أُمَّةٍ أَجَلٌ فَإِذَا جَاءَ أَجَلُهُمْ لَا يَسْتَأْخِرُونَ سَاعَةً وَلَا يَسْتَقْدِمُونَ ﴾ [الأعراف: ٣٤]

"And for every nation is a [specified] term. So when their time has come, they will not remain behind an hour, nor will they precede [it]." [Al-A'raf: 34]

4. When death comes to a believer, the Angel of Death comes to him in a beautiful image, with good fragrance, accompanied by the Angels of Mercy to give him the glad tidings of Paradise. Allah the Most High said,

﴿ إِنَّ الَّذِينَ قَالُوا رَبُّنَا اللهُ ثُمَّ اسْتَقَامُوا تَتَنَزَّلُ عَلَيْهِمُ الْمَلَائِكَةُ أَلَّا تَخَافُوا وَلَا تَحْزَنُوا وَأَبْشِرُوا بِالْجَنَّةِ الَّتِي كُنْتُمْ تُوعَدُونَ ﴾

[فصلت: ٣٠]

"Indeed, those who have said, "Our Lord is Allah " and then remained on a right course - the angels will descend upon them, [saying], "Do not fear and do not grieve but receive good tidings of Paradise, which you were promised." [Fussilat: 30]

As regards the unbeliever, the Angel of Death comes to him in a terrifying image, dark in face, accompanied by the Angels of Punishment, to give him glad tidings of punishment as Allah said,

﴿ وَلَوْ تَرَى إِذِ الظَّالِمُونَ فِي غَمَرَاتِ الْمَوْتِ وَالْمَلَائِكَةُ بَاسِطُو أَيْدِيهِمْ أَخْرِجُوا أَنْفُسَكُمُ الْيَوْمَ تُجْزَوْنَ عَذَابَ الْهُونِ بِمَا كُنْتُمْ تَقُولُونَ عَلَى اللهِ غَيْرَ الْحَقِّ وَكُنْتُمْ عَنْ آيَاتِهِ تَسْتَكْبِرُونَ ﴾

[الأنعام: ٩٣]

The Last Day

And if you could but see when the wrongdoers are in the overwhelming pangs of death while the angels extend their hands, [saying], "Discharge your souls! Today you will be awarded the punishment of [extreme] humiliation for what you used to say against Allah other than the truth and [that] you were, toward His verses [and signs], being arrogant." [Al-An'am: 93]

When death arrives, the truth is uncovered and reality becomes evident to every human. Allah the Most High said,

﴿ حَتَّى إِذَا جَاءَ أَحَدَهُمُ الْمَوْتُ قَالَ رَبِّ ارْجِعُونِ لَعَلِّي أَعْمَلُ صَالِحاً فِيمَا تَرَكْتُ كَلَّا إِنَّهَا كَلِمَةٌ هُوَ قَائِلُهَا وَمِنْ وَرَائِهِمْ بَرْزَخٌ إِلَى يَوْمِ يُبْعَثُونَ ﴾ [المؤمنون ٩٩، ١٠٠]

"Until, when death comes to one of them (those who join partners with Allah), he says: 'My Lord! Send me back, so that I may do well in that which I have left behind!' No! It is but a word that he speaks, and behind them is barzakh (a barrier) until the Day when they will be resurrected." [Al-Mu'minoon: 99, 100] When death arrives, the unbeliever and the insubordinate would feel a keen desire for returning to this life to perform righteous deeds. But nay, it is too late to regret after the opportunity has passed. Allah the Most High said,

$$﴿ وَتَرَى الظَّالِمِينَ لَمَّا رَأَوُا الْعَذَابَ يَقُولُونَ هَلْ إِلَى مَرَدٍّ مِنْ سَبِيلٍ ﴾ [الشورى: ٤٤]$$

"And you will see the wrong-doers, when they behold the punishment, they will say: "Is there any way of return (to the world)?" [As-Shuraa: 44].

5. It is part of Allah's mercy to His slaves that anyone who dies upon proclaiming La ilaaha illa Allaah (there is no deity worthy of worship but Allah) will be admitted to the Paradise. The Messenger of Allah (May the blessings and peace of Allah be upon him) said, "If anyone's last words are "There is no

deity worthy of worship but Allah" he will enter Paradise." [Transmitted by Abu Dawud]

6. This is because one cannot say these words at that difficult period except if he is sincerely devoted. The insincere would find it impossible to proclaim these words owing to the severity of the agony of death he is subjected to. That is why it becomes an act of sunnah for anyone that is present with a person about to die to prompt him to say these words "La ilaaha illa Allaah", according to the saying of the Prophet (may the blessings and peace of Allah be upon him), "Exhort your dying men to recite: 'La ilaaha ill Allah' (There is no deity worthy of worship except Allah)." [Transmitted by Muslim: 916]. This should be done without urgency for him not to get angry and say what is not becoming of him.

The Grave

Anas (may Allah be pleased with him) reported that Allah's Messenger (May the blessings and peace of Allah be upon him) said, *"When the slave of Allah is placed in his grave and his companions retrace their steps, he hears the noise of the footsteps."* He said, *"then two angels come to him and make him sit and say to him: 'What did you used to say about this person (the Prophet?'"* He said, *"As for the faithful believer, he would say: 'I bear testimony to the fact that he is a slave and Messenger of Allah'"*. He said, *"Then it would be said to him: 'Look to your seat in the Hell-Fire, for Allah has substituted it with a seat in Paradise.'"* Allah's Messenger (May the blessings and peace of Allah be upon him) said, *"He would be shown both seats. As for the hypocrite or a non-believer, he would reply, 'I do not know; but I used to say what the people used to say.' So it would be said to him, 'Neither did you know, nor did you follow (i.e. the true path).' Then he will be hit with iron hammers once between his ears, and he will cry a loud cry that everything near him – other than humans and jinn- can hear."* [Transmitted by Al-Bukhari and Muslim: 1338, 2870].

The return of the soul to the body in the grave is from the affairs of the Hereafter, which the human intellect cannot comprehend in this world. However, Muslims have unanimously agreed that a person enjoys bliss in his grave if he were a faithful believer deserving bliss; and that a person will be punished in the grave if he deserves punishment – if Allah does not forgive him. Allah the Most High said,

﴿ النَّارُ يُعْرَضُونَ عَلَيْهَا غُدُوًّا وَعَشِيًّا وَيَوْمَ تَقُومُ السَّاعَةُ أَدْخِلُوا آلَ فِرْعَوْنَ أَشَدَّ الْعَذَابِ ﴾ [غافر:٤٦]

"The Fire; they are exposed to it morning and evening; and on the day when the Hour will be established (it is said): 'Cause Pharaoh's folk to enter the most severe punishment.'" [Ghafir: 46]

The Messenger of Allah (May the blessings and peace of Allah be upon him) said, *"Seek refuge with Allah from the punishment of the grave."* [Transmitted by Muslim: 2867]

Sound reason does not deny this, because one sees in this world some events that bring this reality closer. One who is having a nightmare may feel as if he is being severely punished, and so he shouts and screams seeking aid, while the next person lying close to him does not realize what he feels, despite the great difference between life and death. Both the body and the soul suffer punishment in the grave. Allah's Messenger has said, *"Indeed the grave is the first stage among the stages of the Hereafter. So, if one is saved from it, then what comes after it is easier than it. And if one is not saved from it, then what comes after it is worse."* [Transmitted by At-Tirmidhi: 2230]

Hence, a Muslim should frequently seek refuge with Allah from the punishment of the grave, especially before making *tasleem* in *prayer* (i.e. before concluding the prayer). He should strive to abstain from acts of disobedience to Allah, which are the reasons for deserving punishment in the grave. It has been called the punishment of the grave because most people are buried in graves. However those who drown, burn to death, or are eaten by wild animals, and the like, will all either be punished or granted bliss in the *Barzakh* (the barrier between this world and the Hereafter).

Punishment of the grave varies. It may include: being struck with an iron hammer; the grave may be filled with darkness, or furnished with carpets from Hellfire, or have its gates opened to him; his evil deeds may be shown to him in the form of an ugly man with a foul smell, sitting with him inside the grave. The punishment will be continuous in the case of the disbeliever and hypocrite. As for the sinful Muslim, then the punishment will endure according to his sins, and it may come to an end.

In regards to the faithful believer, he will enjoy bliss in the grave whereby it would be widened for him, filled with light, and a gate will be opened to Paradise from where its good smell and fragrance will come to him. The grave will be furnished from Paradise, and his good deeds will be displayed to him in the form of a handsome man who will give him company in the grave.

Establishment of the Hour and Its Portents

1. Allah did not create this world for us to abide in it forever. A day shall come when it will come to an end. This day is the day when the Last Hour will be established. It is a an indisputable fact, as Allah the Most Glorified and Exalted said,

﴿ إِنَّ السَّاعَةَ لَآتِيَةٌ لَا رَيْبَ فِيهَا وَلَكِنَّ أَكْثَرَ النَّاسِ لَا يُؤْمِنُونَ ﴾ [غافر: ٥٩]

"Indeed, the Hour is surely coming, there is no doubt thereof; yet most of mankind believe not." [Ghafir: 59]

﴿ وَقَالَ الَّذِينَ كَفَرُوا لَا تَأْتِينَا السَّاعَةُ قُلْ بَلَى وَرَبِّي لَتَأْتِيَنَّكُمْ ﴾ [سبأ: ٣]

"Those who disbelieve say: 'The Hour will not come to us.' Say: 'Yes, by my Lord, it will come to you.'" [Saba': 3]

﴿ اقْتَرَبَتِ السَّاعَةُ ﴾ [القمر: ١]

"The Hour has drawn near." [Al-Qamar: 1]

The Last Day

﴿ اقْتَرَبَ لِلنَّاسِ حِسَابُهُمْ وَهُمْ فِي غَفْلَةٍ مُعْرِضُونَ ﴾ [الانبياء:١]

"[The time of] their account has approached for the people, while they are in heedlessness turning away." [Al-Anbiya: 1]

Its proximity is not weighed by human measurement or what we are accustomed to. It is rather something related to the knowledge of Allah, and the period that has elapsed from the lifespan of this world.

Knowledge of the Hour is part of the metaphysical, whose knowledge Allah has exclusively confined to Himself. He did not disclose it to any of His slaves as He said,

﴿ يَسْأَلُكَ النَّاسُ عَنِ السَّاعَةِ قُلْ إِنَّمَا عِلْمُهَا عِنْدَ اللهِ وَمَا يُدْرِيكَ لَعَلَّ السَّاعَةَ تَكُونُ قَرِيبًا ﴾ [الأحزاب:٦٣]

"People ask you concerning the Hour. Say," Knowledge of it is only with Allah. And what may make you perceive? Perhaps the Hour is near." [Al-Ahzab: 63]

The Messenger of Allah (May the blessings and peace of Allah be upon him) has stated signs indicating its nearness and proximity. They include emergence of the false Messiah. This will be a great tribulation for mankind, because Allah, the Most Glorified and Exalted, will grant him power to perform supernatural things by which a lot of people will be deceived. He will order the sky and it will rain, order the pasture and it will grow, bring the dead back to life, and perform other paranormal acts. The Messenger of Allah (May the blessings and peace of Allah be upon him) has stated that he is one-eyed and will bring with him something like Paradise and Hell; but what he calls Paradise will be, in fact, Hell. He will remain on earth for forty days, a day like one year, a day like one month, a day like one week, and the other days like the normal days. No spot will remain on earth except that he will enter it, except for Makkah and Madinah.

Among the portents of the Last Hour, is **the descent of 'Isa bin Maryam (Jesus Christ)** on the white minaret east of Damascus, during the time of Fajr prayer, where he will observe the

The Last Day

Fajr prayer with the people. Then he will seek the anti-Christ and slay him.

Among the signs is **the rising of the sun from its setting point (the west)** whereby people will see it, get scared, and start to believe, but no faith will be of any benefit at that point. There are many other signs and portents of the Last Hour.

2. The Last Hour will be established upon the worst of creation. This is because, prior to this Hour, Allah the Most Glorified will send a good wind that will take away the souls of the faithful believers. When He wishes to eliminate all creatures by death, and put an end to this world, He will command the angel to blow the great horn. When the people hear it, they will collapse (dead). Allah, the Most High, said,

﴿ وَنُفِخَ فِي الصُّورِ فَصَعِقَ مَنْ فِي السَّمَاوَاتِ وَمَنْ فِي الْأَرْضِ إِلَّا مَنْ شَاءَ اللهُ ﴾ [الزمر:٦٨]

"And the Horn will be blown, and whoever is in the heavens and whoever is on the earth will fall dead except whom Allah wills." [Az-

Zumar: 68]. This will happen on a Friday. Thereafter, all the angels will die and none shall remain except Allah the Most Perfect and Exalted.

3. Every human body will perish, and the earth will eat it up except the tailbone, which is a bone in the lower back. The earth will not eat up the bodies of the prophets and martyrs. Then Allah, the Most Perfect, will send down rain from the sky, and the bodies will grow and compose again. When Allah wishes to resurrect the people, he will revive Israfeel, who is the angel in charge of blowing the trumpet. He will blow it for the second time and all creatures will be revived. People will come out of their graves as Allah created them the first time, barefooted, naked, and uncircumcised. Allah the Most High said,

﴿ وَنُفِخَ فِي الصُّورِ فَإِذَا هُم مِّنَ الْأَجْدَاثِ إِلَىٰ رَبِّهِمْ يَنسِلُونَ ﴾

[يٰس: ٥١]

"And the Trumpet will be blown (i.e. the second blowing) and behold! From the graves

The Last Day

they will come out quickly to their Lord."[Ya Sin: 51]

﴿ يَوْمَ يَخْرُجُونَ مِنَ الْأَجْدَاثِ سِرَاعًا كَأَنَّهُمْ إِلَى نُصُبٍ يُوفِضُونَ * خَاشِعَةً أَبْصَارُهُمْ تَرْهَقُهُمْ ذِلَّةٌ ذَلِكَ الْيَوْمُ الَّذِي كَانُوا يُوعَدُونَ ﴾

[المعارج: ٤٣، ٤٤]

"The Day they will emerge from the graves rapidly as if they were racing to a goal. Their eyes humbled, humiliation will cover them. That is the Day which they had been promised!" [Al-Ma'arij: 43-44]

The first person that will be unearthed will be the Seal of the Prophets, our Prophet Muhammad (May the blessings and peace of Allah be upon him), as it was reported from him. Then people will be driven to the assembly ground, which is a broad and plane land. Unbelievers will be gathered to Hell (prone) on their faces. The Messenger of Allah was asked: *"How will the unbeliever be gathered to Hell on his face?"* He replied, *"Is He Who is powerful enough to make him walk on his feet in this world not powerful enough to make him (crawl) upon his face on the Day of Resurrection?"* [Transmitted by Muslim: 2806]

Anyone that turns away from the remembrance of Allah will be raised blind. The sun will draw closer to the creatures, and they will be submerged in perspiration according to their deeds; some up to their knees, some up to their waist, and some will have the sweat going down his throat.

Moreover, there are some who Allah the Most High will give protection with His Shade on the Day when there will be no shade except His Shade. Allah's Messenger said, *"Seven are (the people) whom Allah will give protection with His Shade on the Day when there will be no shade except His Shade (i.e., on the Day of Resurrection), and they are: A just ruler; a youth who grew up upon the worship of Allah; a person* whose heart is attached to the mosque; two *persons who love and meet each other and depart from each other for the sake of Allah; a man whom a beautiful woman of high-rank seduces (for illicit relation)him, but he (rejects*

The Last Day

her offer by saying): 'I fear Allah'; a person who gives a charity and conceals it (to such an extent) that the left hand does not know what the right has given; and a person who remembers Allah in solitude and his eyes pour with tears." [Agreed upon: 1423- 1031]

This blessing is not specific for men, but it also includes women. Every woman will be held to account for her deeds, if they are good then she will be rewarded with good, and if they are bad then she will be rewarded with bad. She will get recompense and judgment just like men.

There will be severe thirst on that day, a day which will last as long as fifty thousand years. However, it will pass for the faithful believer swiftly, like the period spent in the observation of an obligatory prayer.

Then Muslims will arrive at the fountain of the Prophet (May the blessings and peace of Allah be upon him) to drink from it. This fountain is a great honor, which Allah exclusively dedicated to our Prophet (May the blessings and peace of Allah be upon him). His nation will drink from it on the Day of Judgment. Its water is whiter than milk and sweeter than honey. Its fragrance is stronger than the fragrance of musk, and its cups are as many as the stars in the sky. Whoever drinks from it will never feel thirsty again.

People will remain on the assembly ground for a long period waiting for the judgment and accountability to begin. When they had stood and waited long, under that hardship and the intensified heat of the sun, they will seek for someone to intercede for them before Allah to judge between the creation. They will come to Adam (peace be upon him) and he will apologize to them. They will go to Noah (peace be upon him) and he will apologize to them. They will go to Abraham (peace be upon him) and he will apologize to them. They will go to Moses (peace be upon him) and he will apologize to them. They will go to Jesus (peace be upon him) and he will apologize to them. Then, they will come to Muhammad (May the blessings and peace of Allah be upon him) and he will say, *"I am for it."* He will fall down in (prostration) under the Throne and praise Allah with praises which Allah will inspire him on that spot. Then it will be said, *"O Muhammad! Raise your head and ask, for you will be granted (your request); and intercede, for your intercession will be accepted"*. Then Allah will begin the judgment and accountability. The nation of Muhammad will be the first nation to be accounted for its deeds.

Prayer will be the first deed a slave will be held accountable for. If it is found to be sound and acceptable, then his other deeds will be considered, but if the prayer is rejected, all other deeds of his will be rejected. Every slave of Allah will be asked about five things: about his life and what he did with it, about his youth and what he spent it in, about his wealth and how he earned it and how he spent it, and his knowledge and what he did with it.

The first cases that will be judged will be cases related to bloodshed. Retribution on that day will be through good and bad deeds. Part of the good deeds of the one who committed the crime will be taken and given to his opponent. When his good deeds fall short to clear the account, the sins of his opponent will be taken and cast on him.

Then the *siraat* will be set. The *siraat* is a bridge that will be thinner than a hair and sharper than the sword, and it will be set above the Hellfire. People will have to pass over it. Some will pass over it like the twinkling of an eye; some like the passing of the breeze; some like the best kinds of horses; and some will be crawling. On the *siraat* will be pronged hooks that will snatch the unbelievers and cast them into the Hellfire. They and whomever Allah wills among the disobedient believers will fall one after the other into Hell. The unbelievers will be left to abide therein forever, while the disobedient believers will be punished as long as Allah wills, then brought out and taken to Paradise.

Allah will grant permission to whomever He wills among the prophets, messengers and righteous people to intercede for some people admitted into the Hellfire among the people of Tawheed (Unification of Allah) and Allah will take them out of it. Those who have crossed the *siraat*, among the people of Paradise, will stand

The Last Day

on a bridge between Paradise and Hell, where retribution will be administered among them in favor of some. He who has usurped some right belonging to his brother, or has a grievance against him will not enter Paradise until he has taken his revenge against him or gets pardoned by him until they have pure hearts towards one another. When the inhabitants of Paradise enter it, and the inmates of the Hell are taken to Hell, death will be brought forth in the form of a ram and will be slaughtered between Paradise and Hell, while the people of Paradise and Hell watch. Then it would be said, *"O people of Paradise, eternity for you and no death! O people of Hell, eternity for you and no death!"* If anybody could die out of happiness, the people of Paradise would have died out of happiness, and if anybody could die out of sorrow, the people of Hellfire would have died out of sorrow.

Hellfire and Its Punishment

Allah the Most High said,

﴿ فَاتَّقُوا النَّارَ الَّتِي وَقُودُهَا النَّاسُ وَالْحِجَارَةُ أُعِدَّتْ لِلْكَافِرِينَ ﴾

[البقرة: ٢٤]

"Then guard yourselves against the Fire prepared for disbelievers, whose fuel is of men and stones." [Al-Baqarah: 24].

Allah's Messenger said to his Companions, *"The fire which the sons of Adam light up is only one out of seventy parts of the Fire of Hell."* His Companions said, *"By Allah, even an ordinary fire would have been enough (to burn people)."* Thereupon he said: *"It has been given sixty-nine extra portion, each portion is equal to the heat of (the fire in this life)."* [Sahih Al-Bukhari and Muslim: 3265, 2843]

Hellfire is of seven levels. Each level is more severe in punishment than the other. Each level holds people according to their deeds. The hypocrites will be in the lowest depths of the

The Last Day

Hellfire, which is the more severe in punishment. The unbeliever's punishment in the fire will be permanent without interruption. Whenever they get burned, they will be returned to suffer more punishment. Allah, the Most High said,

﴿ كُلَّمَا نَضِجَتْ جُلُودُهُمْ بَدَّلْنَاهُمْ جُلُودًا غَيْرَهَا لِيَذُوقُوا الْعَذَابَ ﴾ [النساء:٥٦]

As often as their skins are consumed We shall exchange them for fresh skins that they may taste the punishment" [An-Nisa: 56]

﴿ وَالَّذِينَ كَفَرُوا لَهُمْ نَارُ جَهَنَّمَ لَا يُقْضَى عَلَيْهِمْ فَيَمُوتُوا وَلَا يُخَفَّفُ عَنْهُم مِّنْ عَذَابِهَا كَذَلِكَ نَجْزِي كُلَّ كَفُورٍ ﴾ [فاطر:٣٦]

"And for those who disbelieve will be the fire of Hell. [Death] is not decreed for them so they may die, nor will its torment be lightened for them. Thus do we recompense every ungrateful one." [Fatir: 36]

They would be shackled therein and their necks would be tied with iron collars. Allah said,

﴿ وَتَرَى الْمُجْرِمِينَ يَوْمَئِذٍ مُقَرَّنِينَ فِي الْأَصْفَادِ ۞ سَرَابِيلُهُمْ مِنْ قَطِرَانٍ وَتَغْشَى وُجُوهَهُمُ النَّارُ ﴾ [إبراهيم: ٤٩-٥٠]

"And you will see the criminals that Day bound together in shackles, their garments of liquid pitch and their faces covered by the Fire." [Ibrahim: 49-50]

The food of the inmates of Hellfire will be *zaqqum*, about which Allah, the Most High, said,

﴿ إِنَّ شَجَرَتَ الزَّقُّومِ ۞ طَعَامُ الْأَثِيمِ ۞ كَالْمُهْلِ يَغْلِي فِي الْبُطُونِ ۞ كَغَلْيِ الْحَمِيمِ ﴾ [الدخان: ٤٣-٤٨]

Verily, the tree of *zaqqum* will be the food of the sinners. Like boiling oil, it will boil in the bellies, like the boiling of scalding water. (It will be said) 'Seize him and drag him into the midst of blazing Fire, then pour over his head the torment of boiling water'". [Ad-Dukhan: 43-48]

To explain the gravity of the punishment of the Hellfire and the greatness of the bliss in Paradise, it was transmitted in Sahih Muslim that the Prophet (may the blessings and peace of Allah be upon him) said, *"The person who had led the most luxurious life in this world, will be brought up on the Day of Resurrection and dipped into the Hellfire. He will be asked, 'O son of Adam! Did you ever experience any comfort? Did you ever experience any luxury?' He will reply, 'By Allah, no, my Lord.' Then one of the people of the Paradise who had experienced extreme misery in the life of this world will be dipped into Paradise. Then he will be asked, 'O son of Adam! Did you ever experience any misery? Did you ever encounter difficulty?' He will say, "By Allah, no, my Lord, I neither experienced misery nor passed through hardship."* [Transmitted by Muslim: 2807].

The unbeliever will forget all the luxury he enjoyed in this world with just one dip in the Hellfire, and the faithful believer will forget all the hardships, poverty and misery he suffered in this world just with one dip into Paradise.

Characteristics and Description of

Al-Jannah (Paradise)

Al-Jannah is the home of eternity and honour, which Allah prepared for His righteous slaves. It involves bliss which no eye has ever perceived, no ear has ever heard of, and no heart has ever imagined. Allah the Most High said,

﴿ فَلَا تَعْلَمُ نَفْسٌ مَا أُخْفِيَ لَهُمْ مِنْ قُرَّةِ أَعْيُنٍ جَزَاءً بِمَا كَانُوا يَعْمَلُونَ ﴾ [السجدة: ١٧]

"No soul knows what is kept hidden for them of joy as a reward for what they used to do." [As-Sajdah: 17]

It is of grades and ranks, whereby the stations of the believers vary according to their deeds. Allah the Most Perfect said,

﴿ يَرْفَعِ اللهُ الَّذِينَ آمَنُوا مِنْكُمْ وَالَّذِينَ أُوتُوا الْعِلْمَ دَرَجَاتٍ ﴾ [المجادلة: ١١]

"Allah will exalt in degree those of you who believe, and those who have been granted

knowledge. And Allah is Well-Aware of what you do." [Al-Mujadalah: 11]

They will eat and drink whatever they desire. Therein are rivers of water unpolluted, rivers of milk whereof the flavour does not change, rivers of clear-run honey and rivers of wine delicious to the drinkers; and their wine is unlike the wine of this world.

﴿ يُطَافُ عَلَيْهِمْ بِكَأْسٍ مِنْ مَعِينٍ * بَيْضَاءَ لَذَّةٍ لِلشَّارِبِينَ * لَا فِيهَا غَوْلٌ وَلَا هُمْ عَنْهَا يُنْزَفُونَ ﴾ [الصافات: ٤٥-٤٧]

"A cup from a gushing spring is brought round for them, White, delicious to the drinkers. Neither they will have pain, from that, nor will they suffer intoxication therefrom." [As-Saffaat: 45-47]

They will be given young virgin women, who do not age, (*Hoor al-'Ein*) as their wives. The Messenger of Allah (May the blessings and peace of Allah be upon him) said, *"And if a woman among the women inhabiting Paradise were to appear to the people of the earth, she would illuminate and fill up what is between the (the heavens and the earth) with light and a pleasant scent.*" [Transmitted by Al-Bukhari: 2796]

The greatest bounty of the people of Paradise is the glance they will have in the face of Allah the most Purified and Exalted. Furthermore, they will neither urinate nor defecate, nor have any other bodily discharge. They will have combs made of gold, and their perspiration is musk. This bounty is permanent, without any interruption or decrease. The Messenger of Allah (May the blessings and peace of Allah be upon him) said, *"He who enters Paradise (will be made to enjoy such an everlasting) bliss that he will neither become destitute, nor will his clothes wear out, nor will his youth decline."* [Transmitted by Muslim: 2836]

The share of the least of the people of Paradise, who will be the last person to leave the Hellfire among the faithful believers and enter Paradise, is ten times better than this entire world.

The Last Day

All praise is due and belongs to Allah, with whose bounty righteous deeds are perfected and accomplished.

Table of Contents

Topic	Page
Legal Rulings Regarding the Last Day	3
Death	5
The Grave	12
Establishment of the Hour and Its Portents	16
Hellfire and Its Punishment	28
Characteristics and Description of Al-Jannah (Paradise)	32

www.ingramcontent.com/pod-product-compliance
Lightning Source LLC
LaVergne TN
LVHW021049100526
838202LV00079B/5410